RECREATION & LEISURE
IN MODERN SOCIETY